# Look at the Animals

by Margie Burton, Cathy French, and Tammy Jones

Look at the grasshopper.

It is green.

It can hide.

3

Look at the fish.
It can hide, too.

5

Look at the snail.
It has a shell.

Look at the tortoise.
It has a shell, too.

Look at the polar bear.
It has fur.

11

Look at the leopard.
It has spots.

Look at the bird.

It has wings.

Look at the bee.

It has wings, too.